FAMOUS FACES IN DARK PLACES

A MENTAL HEALTH BRAG BOOK

GLORIA SHELL MITCHELL

EncourageMint
Books

Gardena, California

© 2019 by Gloria Shell Mitchell
All Rights Reserved

Cover and book design by Samuel Okike (Psalmyy on Fiverr)
Editor: Micheleaust on fiverr.com

Famous Faces in Dark Places is an inspirational piece by
Gloria Shell Mitchell

Other books by Gloria Shell Mitchell include:
The Garbage Man's Daughter Series
Letting Go of Shame
Letting Go of SECRETS
Letting Go of STRESS
Letting Go of SCARS
My Knotty Decision
Bliss and Blisters in Love and Marriage
Desire After Divorce
and
God Says, "I AM"
52 Inspirational Poems and Pieces

Contact
Gloria Shell Mitchell
www.gloriashellmitchell.com
Email: gloriashellmitchell@gmail.com

ISBN-13: 978-0-9761010-4-8

Printed in the United States of America

Disclaimer: All photos, retrieved from random Google images, are copyright properties of their respective owners and have been used for editorial/educational purposes only. Pamphlets will be widely distributed to teach the public about mental illness. An objectionable inclusion will be removed with a revised printing.

DEDICATION

To my late brother, Alexander Shell,
diagnosed with paranoid schizophrenia

To persons diagnosed and undiagnosed

And

To all who are unaware
of the stigma and shame
associated with mental illness

I definitely relate to the poem. Mental Illness can be conquered, but only if one is willing. Not only if one is willing physically, but a lot of mental work has to be done and accomplished with the help of medication. Now, not all medication may be right for you. I have gone through many, many different kinds of medication to find the right levels and mixtures to fit my needs. Yet today I am stable. So it is possible!

Yes doctors can help. But let us not forget the most powerful doctor/physician that exists. That one is called I Am, The Alpha and The Omega. Also known as Jesus Christ of Nazareth.

Many are ashamed of their mental challenge, so they don't seek help. Therefore they reduce themselves to drugs, alcohol, abuse towards self and others and many other harmful activities. There's nothing to be ashamed of! It's common, and like most we are born with it. Please get some help and pray about it. We're here to support as best as we can.

I myself was diagnosed with PTSD, Co-Occurring disorder, Anxiety, Depression, Mood Disorder and ADHD. My racing thoughts DO NOT HELP! I need you as much as you need me. Get help before it's too late.

I enjoyed the way Dr. G has well known people for different categories of mental illness. It showed that mental illness did not stop those who had dreams. Those who had dreams pursued them. If you want to succeed, don't let anything hold you down. Again, you have to work at it though. Its hard work, but good work and worth it!

Celebrity or not, mental illness does not care and can affect anyone! I can relate to numerous of these celebrities. Don't let mental illness take over your life or your mind. There is help out there. You need to do your part and reach out. Dr. G was very informative on diagnoses, how they can be treated and where. A lot of times I felt alone. I felt stuck in my head, like I was the only one with mental illness. After reading this fine piece, I have learned I am not alone. I don't have to stay stuck in my head. There is help out there. There are others out there like me who have indeed succeeded.

Congrats to Dr. G for helping me comprehend the facts of my mental illness that is curable. Now I can rest, knowing I'm not alone.

- Jessica Romero

SPECIAL THANKS and ACKNOWLEDGEMENTS

I thank researchers for sharing that someone commits suicide every 40 seconds and one out of every four persons has a mental illness. These statistics motivated me to put a face on the illness that impacts so many sufferers and the people around them.

This compilation of famous individuals who made mind-boggling accomplishments was prepared to educate, empower, and encourage the diagnosed and the undiagnosed. Like these famous individuals, pursue your dreams, even if they seem impossible to achieve.

Residents at Minnie's Shell, a secure dwelling place for homeless women, provided lived experience with co-occurring disorders. I am convinced that each of them has the potential to accomplish great things if given the opportunity, encouragement and tangible support. Perhaps they will appear in my next brag book.

I give special thanks to the National Alliance for Mental Illness (NAMI) for advocacy, education, and raising awareness. Most definitions and symptoms were obtained from NAMI.org and webmd.com. As a NAMI Family-to-Family facilitator, I have found that education is the key to overcoming the stigma of mental illness.

My graphic designer provided the pictures to put a face on each mental illness. Reviewers with co-occurring disorders provided suggestions for including symptoms and treatment options. Mandatory internship while training as a peer specialist to youth provided exposure to various self-help groups at SHARE! in Culver City, CA. Research for my dissertation on the stigma of divorce provided support groups and other resources where people might find help to combat stigma. The names of famous people came from reading articles, searching the Internet, watching news reports, listening to talk shows and the testimonies of speakers at conferences.

I have included a number of advocates for mental health who have spoken out against the stigma of mental illness. These few (plus countless others) prove that the world has been blessed because of, or in spite of, their illness. As a resident of a traumatized nation in the aftermath of the World Trade Center disaster on September 11, 2001, I consider it a privilege to advocate for mental health.

May you find the contents of this book to be inspirational and user-friendly. If this information pricks your heart, causes you to raise an eyebrow, opens your mind, leads you to say, "Huh?" or prompts you to do your own research, then I have succeeded in raising awareness that your mental health is a valuable asset. Guard it well.

TABLE OF CONTENTS

Depression 13

Seasonal Affective Disorder (SAD) 21

Eating Disorders 22

Dual-Diagnosis Or Co-Occurring Disorders 25

Alcoholism 28

Post-Partum Depression 30

Bipolar Disorder 32

Dyslexia 36

Anxiety And Panic Disorders 38

Social Anxiety Disorder 40

Borderline Personality Disorder (BPD) 42

Dissociative Identity Disorder (DID) 43

Attention Deficit Hyperactivity Disorder (ADHD) 44

Compulsive Buying Disorder (CBD) 45

Hoarding 46

Tourette's Syndrome 47

Schizophrenia 48

Schizoaffective Disorder 49

Autism 50

Post Traumatic Stress Disorder (PTSD) 51

Narcissistic Personality Disorder (NPD) 52
Obsessive-Compulsive Disorder (OCD) 54
Alzheimer's Disease 57
Mental Health Resources 60

FAMOUS FACES IN DARK PLACES

The human brain is a vital body part,
don't you agree?
Why criticize and ostracize sick minds,
when a doctor they should see?

Due to ignorance of signs of mental illness,
great lives have ended in tragedy.
Sufferers have treatment options
and many benefit from therapy.

Whatever mental challenge you face,
someone else has been in that place.
Overcomers discovered creative solutions
and found fame, not disgrace.

Let's take a *Sentimental Journey*
to understand why actor/singer **Doris Day**,
in spite of panic attacks and nervous breakdowns,
"Que Sera, Sera" she could say.

We begin with depression,
no stranger to anyone,
for bouts with debilitating symptoms,
many famous personalities have already won.

NOTE: Nervous Breakdown and Mental Illness

*Nervous or mental breakdown (a term once used to cover a wide range of mental illnesses) describes a period of intense mental distress in which the sufferer is unable to function normally in everyday life. Nervous breakdown, however, is not a form of mental illness. A mental illness is a health condition that changes the way a person thinks, feels and acts. Journey with us as we walk through several forms of mental illness.

DEPRESSION

***Depression** is a common but serious mood disorder that affects how you feel, think, and behave. It causes difficulty with work, study, sleep, eating, relationships, activities and more. Different forms of depression may develop under unique circumstances.*

Abraham Lincoln, the 16th president of the United States, did not allow clinical depression, a nervous breakdown, the loss of 8 elections and two business failures to change his destiny. What a role model for endurance and perseverance!

Television talk show host **Ellen Degeneres** suffered depression when her show was cut after she disclosed being gay.

Actor **Brad Pitt**, star of *The Curious Case of Benjamin Button,* admitted that he smoked too much marijuana while in the dumps, but was jarred to his senses on a trip to Casablanca where the sight of abject poverty inspired him to seek therapy. Oddly enough, fortune and fame can't buy peace of mind. What will it take for you to seek help?

DEPRESSION

Actor and comedian **Jim Carrey**, Golden Globe winner, confessed to struggling with depression at the peak of his career. He became proactive in the fight to prevent medications and substances (i.e., alcohol, drugs, coffee) from affecting his mood.

Artist **Pablo Picasso** painted societal outcasts in somber tones during his Blue Period that revealed his emotional turmoil sparked by the suicide of his friend, Casagemas. He painted Casagemas in His Coffin.

Astronaut **Buzz Aldrin**, the second man to walk on the moon, struggled with the notoriety that came with the success of his mission. There is a downside to fame.

DEPRESSION

Novelist **J. K. Rowling**, creator of Harry Potter, sought help for clinical depression and wrote her way to fame and riches in five years. Help is available if you seek it.

Billionaire talk show host **Oprah Winfrey** was depressed after she adapted, produced, starred in, and bought rights to the box office flop of Tony Morrison's *Beloved*.

Novelist **Virginia Woolf,** author of *To the Lighthouse*, went to the grave after death by suicide.

DEPRESSION

Charles Dickens, author of literary gems *Great Expectations* and *A Christmas Carol*. He experienced mood changes each time he began a new project.

Sigmund Freud, a brilliant neurologist, founded psychoanalysis (analyzing the mind). He is the pioneer in mental health research on the damaging effect of child abuse and neglect and is credited with the discovery that a person could improve by talking to a therapist. Some psychologists believe he suffered from Borderline Personality Disorder because of his notes about experiencing **neurosis** (a class of mental disorders with symptoms of stress). To get relief from his depression, he reportedly abused cocaine.

DEPRESSION

Dwayne "The Rock" Johnson, actor, producer and professional wrestler reached a point where he cried constantly. Realizing that he wasn't alone helped him to get through depression. "Speak up and talk about it" is his advice.

Actor **Angelina Jolie**, Oscar winner, U. N. Goodwill Ambassador, writer, director and mother of many children resorted to self-mutilation in her struggles. Imagine that!

Prince Harry, the Duke of Sussex in the British royal family, suppressed his emotions following the sudden, tragic death of his mother Princess Diana at age 12. Unresolved grief that he could not express went unaddressed and led him to make some bad decisions for about twenty years. Since realizing that his problems affected all the people around him, he now encourages everyone with mental problems to open up and seek professional help.

DEPRESSION

Poet and illustrator **Edward Lear**, who popularized the limerick and wrote the Nonsense poem, *The Owl and the Pussy-Cat* suffered from depression and epilepsy.

Novelist and poet **Leo Tolstoy**-author of *The Three Hermits short story*, often considered suicide before his life changed after becoming a born-again Christian.

Singer **Dolly Parton** attributes most of her depression to menopause and the fact that she never had children. Many unmarried and older women may feel this way.

DEPRESSION

Ludwig van Beethoven, deaf composer of classical music like *Moonlight Sonata*, suffered from depression and bipolar disorder along with too much alcohol.

Innovator **Walt Disney**, creator of Mickey Mouse, was a workaholic who had a nervous breakdown after his wife's miscarriage. He admitted "going to pieces."

Painter, **William H. Johnson**, a poor African American from South Carolina, was sometimes referred to as A Forgotten Harlem Renaissance Artist. His irrational behavior was partly induced by racial discrimination, loss of much of his work in a fire, grief over the death of his wife and the diagnosis of mental illness as the result of syphilis. His series titled Fighters for Freedom is on exhibit in the Smithsonian's American Art Museum in Washington, DC. His last 23 years were spent confined to a mental hospital.

DEPRESSION

60 Minutes correspondent, **Mike Wallace**, allowed a libel lawsuit to push him to attempt suicide. He said, "You're not a nutcase if you want to go see a psychiatrist."

Michelle Williams, singer and mental health advocate (former member of the singing group Destiny's Child), revealed a long battle with depression. African-Americans are most often taught to "just go to church, pray about the problem, trust the Lord and He will heal you." But she urges sufferers to, "Go see a professional so that they can assess you. If you change your mind, you can change your life."

Note: God works through doctors, therapists, counselors, medication, etc. He also works through self-help groups and different types of therapy: talk, music, art, dance, writing, etc. Treatment is essential. Your brain—the most important organ in your body—is responsible for controlling ALL of your bodily functions. Just like you seek professionals to treat a physical illness, you should trust them to treat a mental illness.

Mental illness did not hinder these mind-boggling accomplishments.

SEASONAL AFFECTIVE DISORDER (SAD)

*Seasonal Affective Disorder (SAD) is a form of depression that often occurs during fall and winter, and disappears during spring and summer. It's due to a lack of sunlight. On any given day, you and I may experience this type of depression.

Rosie O'Donnell, talk show host and moderator on The View, shared on the show that if it's sunny in Miami she instantly feels happy, and if it's gray and cloudy, she feels like someone is torturing her. At first she resisted taking prescribed medication, but found it helpful. To everyone afraid of the stigma of medication, she later admitted that medication saved her life.

EATING DISORDERS

Eating disorders are a group of related conditions that cause serious emotional and physical problems. Each condition involves extreme food and weight issues with unique symptoms.

Anorexia Nervosa. People with anorexia will deny themselves food to the point of self-starvation as they obsess about weight loss. With anorexia, a person will deny hunger and refuse to eat, practice binge eating and purging behaviors or exercise to the point of exhaustion as they attempt to limit, eliminate or "burn" calories.

Bulimia Nervosa. People living with bulimia will feel out of control when binging on very large amounts of food during short periods of time, and then desperately try to rid themselves of the extra calories using forced vomiting, abusing laxatives or excessive exercise. This becomes a repeating cycle that controls many aspects of the person's life and has a very negative effect both emotionally and physically. People living with bulimia are usually normal weight or even a bit overweight. The emotional symptoms of bulimia include low self-esteem overly linked to body image, feelings of being out of control, feeling guilty or shameful about eating and withdrawal from friends and family.

Binge Eating Disorder (BED). A person with BED loses control over their eating and eats a very large amount of food in a short period of time. They may also eat large amounts of food even when he isn't hungry or after he is full. This causes them to feel embarrassed, disgusted, depressed or guilty about their behavior. A person with binge eating disorder may be normal weight, overweight or obese. Negative thoughts and habits can trigger overeating. People must be taught how to respond properly to negativity such as emotional pain, conflict, low self-esteem, anxiety, depression, stress or trauma.

EATING DISORDERS

Princess Diana of Wales, a member of the British royal family, the first wife of Prince Charles and mother of Prince Harry and Prince William, spoke openly about her struggles with bulimia and self-mutilation. In a 1995 BBC television interview, the Princess admitted to intentionally cutting her arms and legs. "You have so much pain inside yourself that you try and hurt yourself on the outside because you want help," she said. "I didn't like myself, I was ashamed I couldn't cope with the pressures." Professionals, friends and family helped her to cope with these disorders.

Elton John, singer, struggled with bulimia and undertook a drug treatment program. He said it helped him when he learned that his friend Princess Diana struggled with the same disorder. Share your story. You never know who might be helped by it.

EATING DISORDERS

Katie Couric – first female to become a solo evening newscast anchor, award-winning journalist, best-selling author, entrepreneur. She sought help from a therapist for bulimia.

Kirsten Haglund, crowned Miss America 2008, enrolled in an intensive outpatient treatment for anorexia. She set up a foundation to provide scholarships to persons seeking help for eating disorders.

Mental Illness did not hinder these mind-boggling accomplishments

DUAL-DIAGNOSIS OR CO-OCCURRING DISORDERS

***Dual-Diagnosis** refers to the struggle with a mental disorder and substance abuse. Depression and Substance Abuse often go hand-in-hand as attempts to numb the symptoms lead to addiction. The two illnesses need a dual-diagnosis treatment plan.*

Edgar Allan Poe, father of the American Short Story and author of *The Raven*, suffered from depression and alcoholism.

Billionaire Aviator and film director, **Howard Hughes**, OCD and drug abuser, feared germs and withdrew from the public and became a recluse.

Charlie Parker, was a Jazz saxophonist and songwriter, Grammy award-winner who, with Dizzy Gillespie invented the musical style called bop or bebop. He was committed to a hospital for mental illness, heroin addiction and alcoholism.

DUAL-DIAGNOSIS OR CO-OCCURRING DISORDERS

Playwright, Tony Award-winner and Pulitzer Prize winner **Tennessee Williams**, wrote *A Streetcar Named Desire and Cat on a Hot Tin Roof*. He struggled with depression, alcoholism and his sexuality. He ended up in a mental hospital.

Stephen King, author of 63 books and master of suspense and terror, admittedly wrote *Cujo* under the influence of drugs and alcohol. The intervention of his family and attending Alcoholics Anonymous (AA) meetings helped him.

Oscar De La Hoya- professional boxer, Olympic gold medalist, and ten–time world champion- suffered from depression and addiction to alcohol and cocaine.

DUAL-DIAGNOSIS OR CO-OCCURRING DISORDERS

Rapper and Actor **DMX (Earl Simmons),** whose debut album, *It's Dark and Hell is Hot*, received critical acclaim and commercial success in the first five days of its release, is a bipolar and drug addiction sufferer who talks about the importance of wanting to change the way you live. Are you ready to change?

Mental illness did not hinder these mind-boggling accomplishments.

ALCOHOLISM

***Alcoholism** is a chronic disease that changes the chemistry of the brain causing it to function differently while creating addictive behavior. A chronic disease is one that lasts for three months or more that no vaccine can prevent and no medicine can cure. Treatment is needed.*

Joan Bennett Kennedy, pianist and model, had a form of mental illness and substance abuse. She received an honorary Doctor of Humane Letters degree from Manhattanville College for her ability to emerge victor rather than victim from her marriage to **Senator Edward Kennedy**—an alcoholic and PTSD sufferer. Their son, former congressman **Patrick Kennedy**, an advocate for mental health and himself a recovering alcoholic, wrote in his book, *A Common Struggle*, that the time has come to combat the shame and stigma of an illness that affects so many families like his own.

Author **Ernest Hemingway** – author, poet and Nobel laureate - suffered from bipolar disorder and alcoholism. Life ended in a famous shotgun suicide for the author of *For Whom the Bell Tolls*.

ALCOHOLISM

Alvin Ailey, an African-American male dancer and choreographer with international acclaim, founded the Alvin Ailey American Dance Theater. He struggled with bipolar disorder, drug and alcohol abuse, his sexuality, and the stress of funding a dance company. He had a nervous breakdown and later died of AIDS.

Award-winning actress **Elizabeth Taylor**, known for her rare beauty and multiple marriages, was diagnosed with bipolar disorder and addicted to alcohol.

Ben Affleck, former Batman star, is an actor, writer, director, producer and screenwriter who spoke openly on TODAY about his lifelong struggle with alcohol addiction. He sought treatment for alcoholism at a rehab. "It's about yourself, your life, your family," he said candidly.

POST-PARTUM DEPRESSION

***Post-partum depression** is a severe form of depression related to pregnancy and childbirth in which the mother might feel sad, hopeless, and guilty because she may not feel like she wants to bond with, or care for, her baby.*

Actor **Brooke Shields**, shared her experience in *Down Came the Rain: My Journey with Postpartum Depression.*

Chrissy Teigen, model, television personality, author and wife of multi-platinum recording artist John Legend, says that becoming a mother can be a challenge. After giving birth, she found getting out of bed to get to work on time to be a challenge. She experienced physical pain, loss of appetite, was short-tempered, and easily burst into tears.

POST-PARTUM DEPRESSION

Grammy award-winning artist, **Adele,** said she felt inadequate as a mom and that she had made a terrible decision by giving birth. Instead of taking antidepressants, she connected with other moms who shared her struggles with parenting. We call this type of connection a support group.

Mental illness did not hinder these mind-boggling accomplishments.

BIPOLAR DISORDER

__Bipolar Disorder__ (also known as manic-depression) has a tendency to start in the teen years and early twenties. Bipolar disorder causes unusual changes in energy, mood, activity, and ability to perform daily tasks. A manic episode in which the sufferer is energized is often followed by feelings of sadness, depression and even hopelessness. The condition is similar to **clinical depression** *with depressed mood, loss of pleasure, low energy and activity, feelings of guilt and worthlessness, and thoughts of suicide.*

Jane Pauley, television news anchor for more than 30 years, raised awareness to the disease in her autobiography, *Skywriting: A Life Out of the Blue*.

Mark Twain, Author of *Huckleberry Finn* and *Adventures of Tom Sawyer*, struggled with bipolar and other mental disorders.

BIPOLAR DISORDER

Entrepreneur **Ted Turner**, CEO of Turner Broadcasting Company, founded the first 24-hour cable news network (CNN) and went on to become a philanthropist.

Physicist and mathematician Sir Isaac Newton, who discovered the law of gravitation and three laws of motion that formed the basis for modern physics, suffered from bipolar, autism, schizophrenia, and depression, and had more than one nervous breakdown.

Vincent van Gogh, the post-impressionist painter who greatly influenced 20th century art, struggled with bipolar disorder, schizophrenia, epilepsy, and depression. This great artist cut off his own ear and then painted his portrait showing the bandaged ear. He died at age 37 of what might have been a self-inflicted gunshot wound.

BIPOLAR DISORDER

Singer **Mariah Carey**, who recorded *Emotions,* turned to therapy and medication for bipolar II, a disease that can cause sudden and extreme shifts in mood.

Songwriter Jimi Hendrix, dubbed the greatest electric guitarist of rock music, wrote the song *Manic Depression* after an interviewer said he sounded like a manic- depressive because of his aggression toward people who wronged him and the type of music he produced. He was found dead under strange circumstances at age 27.

Former prime minister of the United Kingdom, **Winston Churchill**, struggled with bipolar disorder and dyslexia, but wrote 43 books while staying up all night writing during periods of high mania.

BIPOLAR DISORDER

Carrie Fisher, author, comedian and actor best known for her role as Princess Leia in Star Wars films, was quite vocal against the stigma of mental illness. Her book *Postcards From The Edge* was a semi-autobiographical work about an actor following a near-suicidal drug overdose and her work at recovery. Recovery is a process, but your life is worth the work.

Mental illness did not hinder these mind-boggling accomplishments.

DYSLEXIA

***Dyslexia** is a learning disability that makes it difficult to read and write due to the way the brain processes graphic symbols. It is a neurological condition that does not affect intelligence.*

Thomas A. Edison, inventor of the light bulb, was an inquisitive child with delayed speech and behavior akin to ADHD in today's children.

Leonardo da Vinci - painter and sculptor, and spearhead of the Italian Renaissance Movement - painted *Mona Lisa, The Last Supper* and other projects.

Entrepreneur and Basketball Hall of Famer **Magic Johnson** changed the way the sport is played and won an Olympic gold medal on the original Dream Team.

DYSLEXIA

Motion picture director **Steven Spielberg**, struggled with schoolwork and bullying, and dropped out of college when offered an internship based on his skillset at Universal Studios. How cool was that for the producer of *Jaws* and *Star Wars*?

Actor **Henry Winkler**, The Fonz in *Happy Days*, is *the* co-author of the *Hank Zipzer* series that chronicles the adventures of a boy coping with dyslexia.

Mental illness did not hinder these mind-boggling accomplishments.

ANXIETY AND PANIC DISORDERS

Anxiety disorders *involve more than temporary worry or fear. It is a normal occurrence for you to be anxious when faced with a problem at work, before taking a test, before a doctor's visit or before making an important decision.*

Anxiety Disorder *refers to when the anxiety does not go away and gets worse over time. The symptoms can interfere with daily activities such as job performance, schoolwork, and relationships.* **Panic Disorder** *relates to recurrent unexpected panic attacks. Panic attacks are sudden periods of intense fear that come on quickly and reach their peak within minutes. These attacks can occur when you least expect them or be triggered by an object or situation.* **Agoraphobia** *often develops after having one or more panic attacks. It can lead to various fears, such as the fear of open spaces and the fear of places where escape is difficult, such as elevators. Agoraphobia can make it difficult for a person to leave their house.*

Paula Deen, TV personality and cooking show host, suffered from Agoraphobia for twenty years. She stayed indoors and cooked for her family as something to do without leaving the house and found cooking therapeutic. She became a stay at home caterer with the help of her sons, and moved on to open restaurants, appear on TV shows, published cookbooks and her memoir, *Paula Deen: It Ain't All About the Cookin'*.

ANXIETY AND PANIC DISORDERS

Kid Cudi, singer, rapper, actor and record producer received almost ten million likes to his facebook post dated October 4, 2016 in which he said, "Yesterday I checked myself into rehab for depression and suicidal urges." Anxiety and depression had prevented him from making new friends, wouldn't allow him to trust anyone, robbed him of his peace. He decided that it was time for him to fix himself. He is to be commended for bravely sharing that he needed help and for taking steps to get it. Do you love others? So what will it take for you to show yourself some love and seek help if needed?

Mental illness did not hinder these mind-boggling accomplishments.

SOCIAL ANXIETY DISORDER

***Social Anxiety Disorder** is a mental illness that produces worry, fear and a constant feeling of being overwhelmed. Though often mistaken for shyness, the sufferer tends to worry about meeting new people, being observed, and performing in front of others. It can interfere with performance, social life, and daily routines such as school, employment, making friends and romantic endeavors. The public careers shown here put the sufferers in a good position to be negatively judged and evaluated.*

Actor, **Chris Evans,** Captain America, is the comic book superhero in movies.

Singer, dancer, actor, talk and game show host **Donny Osmond** is one whose career spans decades.

SOCIAL ANXIETY DISORDER

Quarterback **Steve Young,** National Football Hall of Famer and author of *My Life Behind the Spiral*, led the San Francisco 49ers to the 1995 super bowl victory. Does a star player who is watched by millions in person and on television sound like someone with a problem performing in front of others?

Mental illness did not hinder these mind-boggling accomplishments.

BORDERLINE PERSONALITY DISORDER (BPD)

Borderline Personality Disorder *is characterized by difficulties regulating emotion. That means they feel emotions intensely and for extended periods of time, and find it harder to return to a stable baseline after an emotionally triggering event. This can lead to impulsivity, poor self-image, stormy relationships and intense emotional responses to stressors. Struggling with self-regulation can also result in dangerous behaviors such as self-mutilation (e.g. cutting).*

Brandon Marshall, NFL wide receiver and co-founder of Project 375 (*a* national nonprofit that seeks to end the stigma of mental illness) reminds people that mental illness is treatable. Prior to his diagnosis, he admits to making some bad decisions without knowing why he struggled to control his emotions or manage his life and relationships. He sought medical help and got on a treatment plan. The diagnosis alone made him feel better. If one fourth of all Americans have some type of diagnosable mental illness, it might be a relief to find out the reason for some of your discomfort when you make bad decisions.

DISSOCIATIVE IDENTITY DISORDER (DID)

***Dissociative Identity Disorder (DID)** (formerly known as multiple personality disorder) is most likely caused by several factors, including severe trauma during early childhood (usually extreme, repetitive physical, sexual, or emotional abuse). The sufferer has trouble remembering certain events and exhibits signs of post traumatic stress disorder (PTSD), depression, substance abuse, self-harm or anxiety in an attempt to cope by dissociating the self from a situation or experience that's too violent, traumatic, or painful to assimilate with the conscious self. Almost everyone has experienced mild dissociation, which is like daydreaming or getting lost in the moment while engaged in an activity such as a video game. Dissociative identity disorder is a severe form of dissociation, a mental process that produces a lack of connection in a person's thoughts, memories, feelings, actions, or sense of identity. For someone who has experienced repetitive physical abuse, this sounds like a good way to avoid fear of being tackled in a football game.*

College Football Hall of Famer **Herschel Walker**, former National Football League running back, winner of the Heisman trophy was diagnosed with this disorder. He admitted having played Russian Roulette. You can be at the top of your game, yet in a dark place.

Mental illness did not hinder these mind-boggling accomplishments.

ATTENTION DEFICIT HYPERACTIVITY DISORDER (ADHD)

***Attention Deficit Hyperactivity Disorder (ADHD)** is a chronic condition that affects millions of children and can continue into adulthood. Symptoms include inattention, trouble focusing, being easily distracted, boredom with a task before it's completed, difficulty remembering and following instructions, lack of attention to details or making careless mistakes. Teachers are often quick to observe these symptoms in students.*

Swimmer **Michael Phelps**, winner of 19 Olympic medals, was diagnosed with ADHD at age 9. Swimming provided a way to address his hyperactivity.

Adam Levine, actor, singer, songwriter and judge on NBC's The Voice was unable to sit down, focus and complete schoolwork as a child. When his inability to focus affected his professional career, he sought a treatment plan. "ADHD isn't a bad thing," he said.

COMPULSIVE BUYING DISORDER (CBD)

***Compulsive Buying Disorder (CBD)** is characterized by an obsession with shopping and buying behavior that causes adverse consequences.*

Mary Todd Lincoln, wife of U.S. President Abraham Lincoln and First Lady of the United States, was a compulsive shopper during the country's recovery from the Civil War. After the loss of her children and the assassination of her husband as he sat beside her at the Ford Theatre, she was committed to an insane asylum. Was it grief and loss or some other mental illness that caused her bizarre behavior? Some say schizophrenia while others clearly don't know.

HOARDING

***Hoarding** is a combination of compulsions or behaviors where items are gathered, collected, and stored. Symptoms include the inability to throw things away, difficulty categorizing and organizing them, indecision about what to keep or discard, and feeling embarrassed about all the stuff on hand.*

Pop Artist **Andy Warhol,** who reportedly said, "In the future, everyone will be world-famous for 15 minutes," was a hoarder of everything from receipts to labels on cans. He is said to have written in his journal, "I'd love to have a really clean space."

TOURETTE'S SYNDROME

***Tourette's Syndrome** is one type of Tic Disorder. Tics are involuntary, repetitive movements and vocalizations. Some TS patients possess unique talents and skills, similar to individuals with autism and savant syndrome. (Savant syndrome is defined as a condition in which a person demonstrates capacities or abilities that are greatly in excess to that considered normal.)*

Classical music genius **Wolfgang Amadeus Mozart** suffered from Tourette's syndrome, autism, Asperger's syndrome, ADHD, OCD and other disorders.

Mental illness did not hinder these mind-boggling accomplishments.

SCHIZOPHRENIA

***Schizophrenia** is a chronic and severe mental disorder that affects how a person thinks, feels, and behaves. Schizophrenia may result in some combination of hallucinations, delusions, extremely disordered thinking, behavior that impairs daily functioning, and can be disabling.*

Vaslav Nijinsky, famed male ballet dancer, who revolutionized dance and choreography, suffered from schizophrenia fueled by the stress of managing his own business affairs and bookings. He was institutionalized for most of his life from age 28 till death at 60.

John Nash, winner of 1994 Nobel Prize for Economics, is the renowned mathematician and Professor who spent several years at psychiatric hospitals. His work has provided insight into the factors that govern chance and decision-making. His story of suffering with schizophrenia inspired the movie *A Beautiful Mind*. On May 23, 2015, he and his wife Alicia died in a traffic accident while riding in a taxi on the New Jersey Turnpike.

SCHIZOAFFECTIVE DISORDER

Schizoaffective disorder *is a chronic mental health condition characterized primarily by symptoms of schizophrenia, such as hallucinations or delusions, and symptoms of a mood disorder, such as mania and depression. Schizoaffective disorder can be managed effectively with medication and therapy. Co-occurring substance use disorders are a serious risk and require integrated treatment.*

Charles Joseph "Buddy" Bolden, cornetist, bandleader, and father of Jazz could not read music. Improvising allowed him to play his cornet (similar to the trumpet). By the late 1890s, he led the most successful band in New Orleans and quickly became known as King Bolden, the leading figure of the rising New Orleans-style ragtime music that would later be known as jazz. He complained of headaches, lost his health and his ability to play the cornet and was confined to an insane asylum until his death in 1934 after being accused of attacking two women.

Mental illness did not hinder these mind-boggling accomplishments.

AUTISM

***Autism** is a mental condition common in childhood that is characterized by difficulty in communicating, interacting with others and with repetitive behaviors.*

Albert Einstein, mathematician and physicist, won the Nobel Prize for physics for his explanation of the photoelectric effect. This brilliant engineering instructor and creator of the theory of relativity who did not start talking until age 3 or 4, suffered from autism, schizophrenia, dyslexia, and "Asperger's Syndrome" (a related developmental disorder characterized by higher than average intellectual ability coupled with impaired social skills and restrictive, repetitive patterns of interest and activities).

POST TRAUMATIC STRESS DISORDER (PTSD)

*Post Traumatic Stress Disorder (PTSD) is a mental health problem that can occur after experiencing or witnessing a life-threatening event, a natural disaster, combat, a serious accident, physical or sexual assault, or military sexual trauma (MST). The bombing of the World Trade Center in New York, mass school shootings, terrorism, political uprisings, and the Rodney King Riots left people of all ages traumatized.

Comedian, actor, and talk show host **Whoopi Goldberg** witnessed two planes collide in midair. It's not surprising that she could relate so well to traumatized students in the movie *Sarafina*.

Musician and actor **Lady Gaga**, an anxiety sufferer raped at age 19, speaks out about PTSD.

Mental illness did not hinder these mind-boggling accomplishments.

NARCISSISTIC PERSONALITY DISORDER (NPD)

***Narcissistic Personality Disorder (NPD)** is characterized by self-absorption. The sufferer tends to use and abuse others to get what he or she wants or where he or she wants to go with little or no regard for the feelings of others (a trait seen in sociopaths). Narcissists often believe they are superior to others and may boast about their own importance and abilities. Sufferers focus only on themselves, money and power. They cannot tolerate the slightest bit of criticism and disagreement. Do you know anyone like that?*

Joan Crawford, Academy Award Winner for Best Actress, whose narcissistic abuse of her adopted daughter was dramatized in the movie "Mommie Dearest," based on the book written by her daughter, suffered from NPD.

The Peoples Temple Cult leader, **Jim Jones**, incited the mass suicide/murder of over 900 faithful followers in Jonestown, Guyana. History warns us to beware of those who exploit, belittle, bully and demean others without guilt or shame. Narcissists can wreck your world.

NARCISSISTIC PERSONALITY DISORDER (NPD)

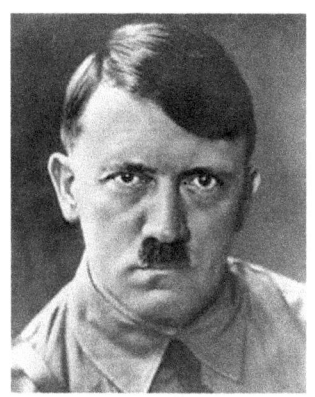

Famous world leaders who made the cut by exhibiting delusions of grandeur include **Adolf Hitler (Germany), Henry VIII (England), Joseph Stalin (Soviet Union), Napoleon Bonaparte (France), Alexander the Great (Greece), Idi Amin (Uganda, East Africa) and Donald Trump (United States of America).** Each has a fascinating story behind his rise to power.

Note: When dealing with narcissists, we must learn not to agitate them, learn how to protect ourselves from their evil words and deeds, and learn how to skillfully navigate around them. This calls for wisdom that comes from God. Pray for wisdom and pray for healing of sick minds. God healed the sick mind of King Nebuchadnezzar of Babylon and he can do it again.

OBSESSIVE-COMPULSIVE DISORDER (OCD)

***Obsessive-compulsive disorder (OCD)** is a common, chronic and long-lasting disorder in which a person has uncontrollable, recurring thoughts (obsessions) and behaviors (compulsions) that he or she feels the urge to repeat over and over.*

Michelangelo - a genius in math and art, painter of the *Sistine Chapel*, sculptor and much more - suffered from OCD and autism.

David Beckham, retired European footballer (soccer star) renowned for his perfectionism on the pitch and famous for his more than 50 tattoos, admits he has to have everything in a straight line, everything has to be in pairs, or everything has to be perfect.

OBSESSIVE-COMPULSIVE DISORDER (OCD)

Charles Darwin published his controversial theory of evolution in the book *On the Origin of Species*, in which he posits that man evolved from monkeys. He struggled with OCD and agoraphobia (extreme fear of crowded spaces or enclosed public places).

Award-winning Actor, **Leonardo DiCaprio**, a mild OCD sufferer, fights the urge to walk through a doorway several times and not to step on every chewing gum stain he sees. While playing the character of OCD sufferer Howard Hughes in *The Aviator*, he realized that he could talk himself out of repetitive urges, whereas hardcore OCD sufferers cannot.

OBSESSIVE-COMPULSIVE DISORDER (OCD)

Nicola Tesla, who developed the alternating current system (AC) and the Tesla coil made incredible advances in early wireless communication. Though one of the greatest minds the world has ever seen, he had rituals he could not avoid. When he stayed in hotels, he insisted on a room number that was divisible by three and demanded that 18 towels be delivered each morning. He needed a neat stack of 18 napkins before he touched his food. He walked around the block 3 times.

The next time you hear about direct current (DC) such as the electricity produced by a battery with positive and negative charges, you might think of the brilliant mind that discovered alternating current (AC). Alternating current makes it possible to build electric generators, motors, and power distribution systems that are far more efficient than DC. AC, the predominant system used globally in high power applications, is the brainchild of a man with OCD.

ALZHEIMER'S DISEASE

***Alzheimer's disease** is a progressive deterioration of the brain and is the primary cause of* **dementia,** *a group of brain disorders that cause the loss of mental and social skills. It is characterized by memory loss (especially short-term), repetitive statements or movements, confusion, the inability to complete simple tasks, problems speaking and writing, losing things, problems finding the right words, and trouble making sound judgments and decisions. Some sufferers do not recognize a spouse of many years.*
Note: Not all seniors contract this disease.

Ronald Reagan, elected the 40th president of the United States at age 69, is credited with ending the cold war between the United States and the Soviet Union. He brought awareness of Alzheimer's Disease to the forefront in November 1994. It is not clear if Reagan's disease was early onset Alzheimer's (which occurs prior to age 65).

ALZHEIMER'S DISEASE

Robin Williams, actor and comedian, who starred in over seventy (70) movies and television series suffered from depression. The official cause of his death was suicide by hanging. After his death it was reported that he suffered from a severe case of dementia with Lewy Bodies (the third most common type of dementia). **Dementia with Lewy Bodies** means you potentially can't think, can't sleep, can't stay awake, can't trust what you see, can't move, can't understand what's going and can't be happy. The world was fortunate to have this star generate years of laughter before the onset of dementia.

Mental illness did not hinder these mind-boggling accomplishments.

What can we conclude from this famous collection?
Though all made a lasting impact on society,
too many famous faces in dark places
chose to bail out of life's agony.

Awareness is key to breaking
barriers of stigma and shame.
These few overcomers represent many
who gained fortune and fame.

May their accomplishments
encourage you to value your mental health.
Knowledge is power,
and possession of it, intangible wealth.

MENTAL HEALTH RESOURCES

Direct Services

Your local crisis response services**Call 911**
Call if you or someone you know is in danger of harming the self, him/herself or someone else

NAMI Helpline Call (800) 950-6264 or, if in Crisis, Text NAMI to 741741
Provides peer support, information and advocacy for family and friends

National Suicide Prevention Lifeline**Call 800-273-8255 (24 Hrs)**

Contact your regular doctor or health care provider _____

Self-Help Groups

Adult Children of Alcoholics/Dysfunctional Families (ACA) www.adultchildren.org
Helps people heal from effects of growing up in a dysfunctional family

Adult Survivors of Childhood Abuse (ASCA) www.ascasupport.org
For adult survivors of neglect, physical, sexual, and/or emotional abuse

AL-ANON www.al-anon.org
Teaches family members of addicts to be supportive but "detach with love"

ALATEEN & PRETEEN www.al-anon.alateen.org/for-alateen
Serves young people dealing with any family dysfunction, plus alcoholism

Alcoholics Anonymous (AA) www.aa.org
The original 12-step program started by upper middle class Protestants

A. R. T. S. Anonymous www.artsanonymous.org
A 12-step recovery path that releases artists to use their creative gifts

Celebrate Recovery (CR) www.celebraterecovery.com
Christian program to help participants overcome hurts, hang-ups, and habits

Because I Love You (BILY) www.bily.org
Helps improve communication and healthy boundaries in families

Bereavement Groups are found in most assisted living facilities and senior centers

Center for Victims of Torture (CVT) www.cvt.org
For victims of torture including refugees and asylum seekers

Cleptomanics and Shoplifters Anonymous (CASA) www.kleptomaniacsanonymous.com (For persons addicted to adrenaline.)

Clutterers Anonymous www.cluttersanonymous.org
Deals with any clutter—physical, emotional or mental

Cocaine Anonymous (CA) www.ca.org
A meeting where addicts, many who are professionals, talk about any substance

Co-Dependents Anonymous (CODA) www.coda.org
For anyone who wants healthy relationships with others and themselves

COSA www.cosa-recovery.org
For men and women affected by someone else's sexual addiction

Compassionate Friends www.compassionatefriends.org
A non-12-step grief support group for anyone who has lost a child or others

Compulsive Eaters Anonymous HOW (CEA-HOW) www.ceahow.org
Addresses eating disorders such as overeating, anorexia, and bulimia

Crystal Meth Anonymous www.crystalmeth.org
Addresses any amphetamine use

Debtors Anonymous (DA) www.debtorsanonymous.org
Deals with credit card debt and any money issues, plus credit restoration

Depression & Bipolar Support Alliance (DBSA) www.dbsalaca.org
For anyone with a mood disorder

DivorceCare www.divorcecare.org
   Participants receive help through separation and divorce (via meetings and online)

Dual Diagnosis Anonymous www.dualdiagnosis.org
   Handles co-occurring mental health conditions and substance use disorders

Dual Recovery Anonymous (DRA) www.draonline.org
   Distinguishes between taking drugs to get high and taking prescription drugs

Emotions Anonymous (EA) www.emotionsanonymous.org
   For any mental health issues and allows people to tell their stories

Families Anonymous (FA) www.familiesanonymous.org
   Offers a Tough Love approach wherein parents kick their kids out who use drugs

Food Addicts Anonymous (FAA) www.foodaddictsanonymous.org
   The disease of food addiction is addressed by abstaining from white sugar

Free N One www.free-n-one.org
   Christian program that helps with jobs and housing to maintain sobriety

Free N One Tough Love Support Group
   For loved ones of addicts and alcoholics in Free-N-One

GAM-ANON www.gam-anon.org
   A program for people affected by compulsive gamblers

Gamblers Anonymous (GA) www.gamblersanonymous.org
   Participants engage in a range of risky behaviors such as shoplifting, street racing

Hearing Voices www.hearingvoicesusa.org
   For persons hearing voices, seeing visions, having other extreme experiences

Male Survivors of Sexual www.malesurvivor.org
   Addresses abuse, assault and trauma of sexually betrayed men and boys

Marijuana Anonymous www.marijuana-anonymous.org
   Formed because marijuana addiction wasn't seen as a serious problem

Mental Health America http://www.mentalhealthamerica.net/find-support-groups
(Online support groups

Millati Islami www.millatiislami.org
An Islamic 12-step program for persons with problems of addiction

Moderation Management www.moderation.org
Helps problem drinkers who don't consider themselves to be alcoholics

Nar-Anon www.nar-anon.org
Support for family and friends of members of Narcotics Anonymous

Narcotics Anonymous (NA) www.na.org
The focus is on the addiction rather than the particular substance

National Alliance for Mental Illness (NAMI) www.nami.org
Provides peer support, information and advocacy for family and friends

National Center for Men http://www.nationalcenter-formen.org/page25.shtml
Fighting for fairness and equal rights for divorced dads

National Center for Post Traumatic Stress Disorder (PTSD)
https://www.ptsd.va.gov/public/treatment/cope/peer_support_groups.asp

Neurotics Anonimos (N/A) www.neuroticsanominos.us
Views self-centeredness as the root of emotional ills and love as the healer

Nicotine Anonymous (NiCA) http://nicotine-anonymous.org
Abstinence from any form of nicotine—smoking, chewing gum, snuffing, vaping

On-line Gamers Anonymous
For those healing from video game and internet addiction

Overcomers Outreach www.overcomersoutreach.org
Christians attend 12-step meetings during the week and share their faith

Overeaters Anonymous http://oa.org
For people who use food as a drug

Parents and Friends of Lesbians and Gays (P-FLAG)
www.pflag.org
> Peer support, information, and advocacy for LGBTQ families

Peace Over Violence www.peaceoverviolence.org
> Dedicated to building healthy relationships, families and communities free from sexual, domestic and interpersonal violence

Pills Anonymous www.pillsanonymous.org
> Members have become addicted to prescription pills

Rainbows https://rainbows.org/
> Helps children and teens grieve and grow after a family trauma like divorce

Recovering Couples Anonymous www.recovering-couples.org
> A 12-step group for persons in a committed relationship

Recovery International www.recoveryinternational.org
> For mental health of people who need to manage their reactions and emotions such as people in bad marriages, vets with PTSD, disobedient wives

Refuge Recovery www.refugerecovery.org
> Freedom from uncontrollable thirst or repetitive craving through meditation

SMART Recovery www.smartrecovery.org
> Self–management for addiction recovery changes "stinking-thinking"

S-ANON www.sanon.org
> Companion to SA, often attended by wives of men who have affairs

Secular Organizations for Sobriety (SOS) www.sossobriety.org
> A non 12-step alternative to AA that appeals to atheists and Bhuddists

Sex Addicts Anonymous www.saa-recovery.org
> Addresses sex with strangers, excessive masturbation, pornography

Sex and Love Addicts Anonymous (SLAA) www.slaafws.org
> Members deal with being in love as a drug as well as an addiction to sex

Sexaholics Anonymous (SA) www.sa.org
> The goal is to stop lusting and become sexually sober (Mostly married men)

Sexual Compulsives Anonymous (SCA) www.sca-recovery.org
Mostly gay men who create their own "Bottom Line" for sexual behavior

Sex and Porn Addicts Anonymous (SPAA) www.spa-recovery.org
Defines abstinence as no porn, no self-sex, and no sex outside a relationship

Sexual Recovery Anonymous (SRA) www.sexualrecovery.org
Mostly consists of gay men who define their own sexual abstinence

Survivors of Incest Anonymous (SIA) www.siasocal.org
A 12-step program that defines childhood sexual abuse as any hurtful actions

Survivors of Those Abused by Priests (SNAP) www.snapnetwork.org
Provides advocacy efforts on behalf of those abused by priests

Taking Off Pounds Sensibly (TOPS) www.tops.org
Encourages weight loss by members following their doctor's meal plan

Underearners Anonymous www.underearnersanonymous.org
Teaches people to pursue their dream job with a prosperity vision

Workaholics Anonymous www.workaholicsanonymous.org
Members learn to stop using work to suppress feelings or avoid problems

Written Material

Diagnostic and Statistical Manual of Mental Disorders (DSM)
The **DSM-V** is the standard classification of mental disorders used by mental health and other health professionals, and is used for diagnostic and research purposes.

And

The
HOLY BIBLE

www.ingramcontent.com/pod-product-compliance
Lightning Source LLC
Chambersburg PA
CBHW061248040426
42444CB00010B/2306